Lawson Stewart Publishing

Ocala, FL

Copyright © 2012 by James S. Bain

ISBN-10: 0985836806

ISBN-13: 978-0-9858368-0-1

Dedications

To Dad: I am so blessed to have had you for a father. Even more special, I am honored to have had you for a teacher and a friend. I will just have to trust that somewhere in Heaven, at some time, you'll get a chance to read it.

To Mom: Throughout my life, and most especially in the early years on which so much of this book is based, I could not have asked for a more loving and supportive Mom. Thank you for being my biggest fan.

And, to my older brother Don, who continues to be an inspiration to me more than 30 years after his passing.

This is for all of you.

Never Pass on a Chance to P!

Never Pass on a Chance to P!

Contents

Chapter 4: Priorities

Chapter 5: Persistence

Chapter 6: Success

Acknowledgements

Many thanks to:

Susie Wood, illustrator extraordinaire. Susie was always ahead of me and gently nudging me forward.

Elizabeth Waller, copy editor and friend. While we don't agree on some things, we did agree on this finished product.

Zoë Christopher, friend. Zoë was there in the earliest days of the project, reading my first stories and encouraging the muse in me.

J.J. Crampton, also a friend, was there in the early days, encouraging, laughing, and pushing, all at the same time.

My *Scenic Overlook* readers and the Meadow Wood Farms residents for reading my newsletters and ramblings. Your encouragement was a much needed boost when I got bogged down in the project.

Merry Lee Bain, my loving wife. You have heard these stories over and over. Thanks for listening again and again.

Never Pass on a Chance to P!

Preface

There are three kinds of men. The one that learns by reading. The few who learn by observation. The rest of them have to pee on the electric fence for themselves. – **Will Rogers**

There are lots of "self-help" books out there. They're written by people like Norman Schwarzkopf, Mike Krzyzewski, Lee Iacocca, and Jack Welch. They're written about people like Jesus, Abraham Lincoln, and the Dalai Lama.

This is not one of those books.

It has been written by a regular guy, who has lived a regular life (admittedly very blessed), and who has learned some very valuable lessons, mostly from his very regular father.

In short, it is a book of practical advice. *Never Pass on a Chance to P* is a compendium of advice, admonishments, and simple instructions that I wish I had understood when I first heard them. Maybe I'm just like my own kids. Maybe I never really learned anything until I made the mistakes and looked back and said "oh yeah, Dad told me that once." Maybe the legendary basketball coach, John Wooden, was right when he said, "It's what you learn after you know it all that counts."

Never Pass on a Chance to P!

Apparently, I never listened to my father, or anybody else with any sense. Maybe you didn't either. Some of the mistakes I have made have been nothing short of monumental. And maybe, Will Rogers was right and this is a fruitless effort to pass along lessons never really learned through stories. Maybe we can only learn these things through trial and error. If nothing else, I hope that you enjoy the journey, see yourself in some of the situations, and remember that we are never too old to learn.

Never Pass on a Chance to P!

Introduction

Why are you here, on this planet, at this time? What significance does your life have? What do you really want from life? Whether you are a philosopher, a spiritual leader, a highly educated university professor, a rocket scientist, a salesman, an auto mechanic, or a ditch digger, you may have asked yourself one or more of these questions. The bookshelves of libraries and bookstores around the world are crammed with books that attempt to help you answer your questions about your life. Many are filled with psychological data, research that will make your head spin, and theories that may make sense to some, but often not to what I would call "normal" people – people like you and me.

Much of what you read may be helpful, but little of it gives you practical advice on how to live your life, simply and easily, to attain that peace for which so many of us search. Folks, in my humble opinion, it's just not that difficult. It's as simple as *Never Pass on a Chance to P!* Now *that* is a catchy name for a simple principle.

Start with a Purpose. Prepare yourself, physically, mentally, emotionally, and spiritually for whatever path you choose to take. Involve yourself with the right People. While your individual talents and efforts will position you to succeed, it is the people with whom you surround yourself that will both reflect and amplify that success.

1

Learn to set Priorities based upon your Purpose. You will spend the majority of your time on this earth doing what is most important to you. Spend that time intentionally on the things you care about most – your family, friends, co-workers, and neighbors. Contribute. Be Persistent. Life isn't easy. It takes practice, mistakes, effort, and a willingness to get up and try again when you get knocked down. Do these five things and your success is the ultimate result. It is the ultimate reward for life on planet Earth.

So there they are, Purpose, Preparation, People, Priorities, and Persistence. Done well, they will lead to Success and Happiness – for you. Focus on these five things and you, too, can find a truly rewarding life. NEVER pass on a chance to P!

Your Roadmap to Success

The chapters of this book are intended to illustrate that framework. For the most part, they are lessons from my father, mother, and older brother. You will find stories and examples from these regular people that demonstrate the principles of Purpose, Preparation, People, Priorities, and Persistence. You will not find in-depth research, highbrow theory, or deep philosophical thoughts. You will find practical advice on how to make your life easier and more rewarding. You will be able to create your own roadmap for your success and happiness.

You may be doing some of the things we suggest in this book already. Just as taking a road trip requires that you know where you are, where you are going, and how you plan to get there, the keys to your roadmap for success are understanding what you are doing, knowing why you are doing it, and visualizing what the results can be. Awareness is at least half the battle. The rest is up to you. Good luck and safe travels.

SUCCESS

To laugh often and much;
to win the respect of intelligent people
and the affection of children; to earn the
appreciation of honest critics and
endure the betrayal of false friends;
to appreciate beauty; to find the best
in others; to leave the world a bit
better, whether by a healthy child,
a garden patch or redeemed
social condition; to know even
one life has breathed easier because
you have lived. This is to have
succeeded.

-Ralph Waldo Emerson

Chapter 1

PURPOSE

"The only true gift is a portion of thyself." – Ralph Waldo Emerson

Purpose

Never Pass on a Chance to P –

Never pass on a chance to pee! I learned this lesson
as a young boy, traveling around the eastern United
States on camping vacations with my parents. I grew
up in West Lafayette, Indiana, a small Midwestern
college town, with Midwestern friends, Midwestern
values, and a series of Midwestern lessons that seem
to have had the same long term effect on me as the
familiar smell of the black farm soil in the early
summer. I can't get those lessons out of my head any
better than I can get that wonderful smell out of my
head. The smell of that dirt has meaning for me even
today. It reminds me of my childhood. It reminds me
of the values with which I was raised. It reminds me
that most of the really important lessons in my life
literally sprouted, took shape, and grew in the
Midwest.

My father was a businessman at a time when there
were only a few types of people living in West
Lafayette. In those years, the kids who lived in West
Lafayette had dads who seemed to do one of very few
things. They were doctors, lawyers, or professors at
Purdue. It seemed to me that no one's dad was *just* a
salesman. But my Dad was. He sold insurance. As an
insurance salesman, he was very good at recognizing
and capitalizing on opportunities. He seemed to
think that only a limited number of opportunities
come your way in life and that you should be
prepared to take advantage of every one you could.

7

Purpose

In my house, there was no "luck." Luck was where preparation met opportunity.

Because both Mom and Dad came to Indiana from the East Coast, we traveled back east every vacation we had. In fact, my earliest memories of vacations included a station wagon, two brothers, and a pop-up camper we borrowed from a family friend. We, like many other families of the day, would load into the station wagon, complete with a comfy sleeping bag arrangement in the "back-in-the-back" for kid road naps and off we would go. We would stop when we needed gas. We would stop when we could find a road side rest area to pop open the fridge in the camper, throw a few sandwiches together, and share a family meal. We would stop at a campground for a night or two while experiencing the history of the Eastern U.S. We went to Fort Ticonderoga, Williamsburg, Virginia, Mystic Seaport in Connecticut, the coast of Maine, New Jersey, Philadelphia. You name it, we saw it. By golly it was a vacation, but the boys were going to *learn* something.

Each time we stopped, at a gas station, a rest stop, a campground, or a historical site, we would do what all kids do. We explored. We climbed boulders as big as buildings in the parks and campgrounds. We climbed the walls of Fort Ticonderoga. We fought each other for the chance to look through those large "scenic view" binoculars mounted on posts along the sides of the road.

Purpose

Whenever Dad decided it was time to go, he would always say, "Who needs to pee?" As a young boy, I was torn between taking that last chance for a bathroom break, or giving up my best shot at being first into the station wagon to claim my seat or my spot in the back-in-the-back. Do I pee, or do I race my brothers to the car to be sure of the best seat? What would you have done? You betcha, I passed on my chance to pee to claim my seat. Now I know that Dad was trying to prevent an unnecessary stop 20 minutes later. And I learned, pretty quickly I might add, that really having to pee and making Dad mad by asking him to stop was not a desirable choice either. Dad was not just upset because he was inconvenienced. And while he didn't verbalize it at the time, he was teaching us to recognize when an opportunity presents itself. He was teaching us to take advantage of that opportunity while it was there. He was teaching us to make good choices.

You may have heard the same lesson said this way, made popular in the Robin Williams film, *Dead Poets Society*: "Carpe Diem." It's Latin for "seize the day," or, never pass on a chance to pee – I'm not sure which. Every new day is an opportunity. It is an opportunity to pursue your purpose, to prepare yourself for success, to surround yourself with the right people, to focus on your priorities, and to persist until you reach your goals for that day. Every day is also full of opportunities. You need only to

Purpose

know that they are there, waiting for you to come along and take advantage of them.

You have the opportunity, today, to stop and seize the day, take the chance to pee, to learn how you can find the life you've been looking for, be blissfully happy, and to know why you are here. It is a choice you make. Choose wisely.

> **Tip:** Look for opportunities in the ordinary. Smile at someone. Pay a compliment. The opportunities are there, just waiting for you to discover them.

Purpose

Start with the Man in the Mirror –

It has been said that we can only change the world one person at a time. On your journey to happiness and success, however you define them, it all starts with you. Every day, when you look at yourself in the mirror, you should be asking yourself some questions. Am I the person I can be? Am I the person I want to be? How does my presence on this earth make a difference? The answers to these questions lie not in our long term goals, although we certainly need goals. The answers lie in what we intend to do *today* to make someone else's life a little easier.

While I hadn't heard the expression in my younger years, I have come to know that people are usually wearing a metaphorical bib or a metaphorical apron. That is, they want or need to be served or they want or need to be of service. As I look back at both my Dad and my Mom, they were servants. As an insurance agent, Dad was in the service business. But, his service to others went well beyond his business life. He began his adult life in the service of his country, a pilot in the U.S. Navy. That experience alone had an impact in the future by encouraging both my older brother Don and me to enter the Navy and the U.S. Air Force, respectively. It was something that Dad was proud of and subsequently, something we were proud of, too.

Dad served as the Treasurer of our church. He served on the hospital Board of Directors. He served

as an assistant leader of our Boy Scout troop. He was
on the local school foundation board. Over the years
he served on the Boards or committees of countless
organizations, lending both his diplomatic skills and
his technical knowledge of the insurance market to
group after group. He never wore any of these roles
on his sleeve. He just did them out of a self imposed
obligation to be of service.

Dad never talked about his service much, so when I
actually got to see him in action, I was one proud kid.
Every year, our local high school staged a chicken
barbecue followed by the pre-season inter-squad
football game. It was a huge community event with
the proceeds directed toward the entire athletic
program. As young kids, we looked forward to it for
weeks before it actually happened. Everybody would
be there. Kids would be running around, playing
touch football. Adults would be chatting, trying to
discipline their kids, and eating wonderful chicken,
corn on the cob, and watermelon. It was a feast, a
party, and a football game all rolled into one. As we
got older, and started to play football, we got even
more excited. To this day, I can picture Dad,
standing behind one of the big barbecue grills,
dressed in a white apron, covered with barbecue
sauce. I'm sure that some years he helped in less
conspicuous ways, but what I remember is the apron.

It's funny. Dad did those things because he felt as if
it was the right thing to do. Serving others came
naturally to him – and Mom. They had no idea of the

impact that they might have for years to come on everyone they touched. Years later, I found myself doing many of those same things. I think my favorite "apron" was the one I wore as the head coach of Little League football teams over the course of ten years. I wonder how many of the roughly 250 kids that went through our program (now adults) look back and remember their little league football coach – me – and understand that success and happiness in life comes from serving others.

I've learned from my Dad and my Mom that we will impact everyone we touch. We can no more choose whether we will have an impact on someone than a pebble can choose whether it will cause a ripple when tossed into the water. We can only choose whether our impact will be a positive one or a negative one. Our best chance at ensuring a positive impact is to commit ourselves to service. We must commit to wearing an apron rather than a bib.

> **Tip:** Every morning, as you prepare for your day, look into the mirror and ask yourself this question. How, today, will I leave every person, place, or thing, better than I found it? How can I be of service, today?

Purpose

Play Golf – Then Count the Money

I suppose that Dad was predestined to fall in love with golf. He was born a Scotsman, and spent his entire career in the insurance business, two almost genetic predispositions for playing the game. He once told me about a friend of his who was interviewing with the Insurance Company of North America (known as INA in those years), as was Dad. They were both hoping to land jobs as field agents for the company, basically traveling a territory and working with independent insurance agents to encourage them to use INA. His friend was asked why he wanted to work for INA – and this is what he said:

> "Well, I grew up on a country club golf course. I noticed as a kid that the only people who seemed to be playing golf were doctors, lawyers, and insurance salesmen. I'm not smart enough to be a doctor. I'm too honest to be a lawyer. I want to play golf, so I figured I'd better get into the insurance business."

They hired him on the spot. Fortunately, my Dad was hired too, although I'm sure it wasn't because of any clever responses. And, he began to play a fair amount of golf. Over the years, he became pretty good at it. He played on weekends and usually on men's day. Golf was his passion. I, too, have learned and become passionate about the game. It is mentally challenging, socially advantageous, and a chance to get some good fresh air. More than that,

golf is a great metaphor for life. Many of the lessons I learned from Dad are rooted in the game of golf.

For so many of us, our measure of success is somehow tied to the homes we own, the cars we drive, the size of our bank accounts, or the clubs we belong to. One of Dad's (and golf's) lessons is to play golf, then count the money. It's a simple concept, really. Focus on the fundamentals and the results will take care of themselves. In golf, those fundamentals might be stance, grip, balance, and tempo. The fact is, that if those things are not done right, the results are often shots deep into the woods, skittered off the tee, or dumped into the lake. Awful at worst, troublesome at best. Not focusing on the fundamentals will not always give you a miserable result, but it will more often than not.

So, how can we improve our results in life? Focus on the fundamentals! The fundamentals in our lives are not all that difficult to understand. Much like the game of golf, they may be hard to master, but they are not hard to understand.

Let's start with the fundamental of service. We, as human beings, are social animals. Much like horses, dogs, ants, or bees, our purpose on this planet is to serve the herd, the pack, the hill, the hive. We are here to serve our fellow man, to make his or her life a little easier. It doesn't matter whether you are a worker bee or the queen bee, a mare or a stallion, your primary purpose is to use your God given talents to protect, preserve, and perpetuate your group. When we begin to understand that giving is truly more satisfying than receiving, we are on our way to understanding one of the basic fundamentals of our existence. We are beginning to understand our purpose.

As with everything else in life, following this purpose requires that we make choices. We must choose the welfare of the group over our own. We must choose to serve one another before serving ourselves. We must choose to wear an apron, rather than a bib.

If we make the right choices, we are on our way to a truly happy life. We can know that at the end of the day, we will be enriched in so many ways. We have focused on the fundamentals and the results have taken care of themselves. We have played golf, and we can count the money later.

> **Tip:** Perform a random act of kindness every day. It will help whoever you choose as the recipient of that act and will make you feel good in the process.

Purpose

The World is Run by C Students –

Of course not all of my life's lessons have come from
my father. In fact, a great many of them have come
from the regular people I've had the good fortune to
meet and get to know in my life. One such man was
my former father-in-law. Stormy was a big, strong,
athletic, and jovial guy. Standing about 6'3" and
weighing about 235, he was an imposing man. He
had been a track and football star in high school and
went on to play both college and professional football
for the then Baltimore Colts. In the early 1950's he
was that rare combination of both size and speed. As
I was the first to marry one of his three daughters,
he was both intimidating and kind. I knew that he
accepted me as his daughter's choice for a husband,
but I also knew that he was not a man to be trifled
with.

Like my father, he too was "just" a salesman. As a
star athlete, he had had his share of recognition and
adulation. But as a salesman, he had to sharpen his
other considerable skills to be successful. He had not
been the best of students but was nonetheless an
intelligent and hard working guy. He knew the value
of working hard and taking care of his customers. He
knew the value of caring for his family. He knew the
value of serving others rather than himself.

A fundamentally humble man, he would often say,
"the world is run by C students." I suspect that he
wasn't necessarily referring to the President of the

United States or the Prime Ministers of England, France, or Canada, or the President of Mexico, or the head of the World Bank. I suspect that he was referring to those who do the actual work, make things happen, and work their way to the top of their companies, their professions, or their teams. I suspect that part of what he was saying is that what makes the world go around are regular people.

I know he wasn't suggesting that those who are "running the world" are less than talented, less than intelligent, less than productive. He was suggesting, and accurately so, that no matter how well we may or may not have done in school, there is an incredible opportunity out there for all of us, whether we are the average Joe, or the star player. I believe that the other point he was making was that one should never be intimidated by a title or position. The people with the big titles are usually just regular people too. Like you, they have worked hard, taken full advantage of their opportunities, made many mistakes, and learned along the way. As the saying goes, they put their pants on one leg at a time, just like you do.

As an example, I have had the good fortune to work with the construction industry, in one way or another, throughout my career. There are several things about the construction industry that make it unique in our economy. The industry provides one of the best opportunities to start as a production worker, a craftsperson, work your way up in an organization, and become a principal, or start your own business. It is a model for the "American Dream." And, it is largely populated with regular people, the "C students," who have earned their way to the top through hard work and knowing the value of serving the customer and the construction team. This, I think, is the "world" my father-in-law was talking about – your world, your life, your profession.

And what is your opportunity? No matter what your chosen profession might be, we all have the opportunity to affect the lives of those we encounter, through our work, through our family, through our friends. Grades don't matter. Wealth doesn't matter. Fame doesn't matter. What matters is leaving your world a little better than you found it. And that choice is always yours.

> **Tip:** "Never believe that you are better than anybody else, but remember that you're just as good as everybody else. That's important: No better, but just as good!" – John Wooden

If You Want Something Badly Enough... –

Dad was never one to sit down in his chair and pontificate. I don't ever recall him sitting us down and giving us any fatherly advice. He just continued to say and do things that would ultimately serve as our model for living. One of the things he repeated anytime we "wished" we could have this or that was, "if you want something badly enough, be patient. You will find a way to get it."

I guess he had some confidence that our means to get whatever it was we were pining for would be honorable. Again, he led us much more by example than by word. But he was also confident that we would come to the realization that we needed to set goals for ourselves, even if those goals were typical of kids and were more about stuff than substance.

I had turned 16 that summer and had been working summers since I was 14. I wasn't a great saver of money and had a tendency to save just enough to buy the next thing that I really wanted. My first purchase with my summer job money had been a Sony cassette tape deck, amplifier and speakers, but that was when I was 14. This summer, I wanted a car! I announced as the summer approached that I wanted to buy a car with my summer earnings. Dad didn't discourage me in any way. He did point out that the ongoing costs of gas, maintenance, and insurance might require that I continue to work during the school year. When he saw the somewhat

Purpose

overwhelmed look on my face, he simply looked at me and said, "if you want something badly enough..." I knew what he meant. I was going to have to figure it out, make a plan, and really go after what I wanted. He simply wanted me to be realistic and smart about it.

The summer wore on and day after day, I would get a ride to work from one of my friends. I worked for the city street department that summer, riding around in the back of a dump truck and picking up anything the garbage guys couldn't - or wouldn't - take. Sometimes it was an old couch, a lawnmower that no longer ran, or, all too often, some unfortunate critter that had become roadkill and needed to be removed from the street with a pitchfork and scoop shovel. It was a GREAT job!

As the summer neared its end and football practice loomed, I had earned a nice chunk of change. I had nearly $500 to spend and was feeling pretty good about myself. Then we started looking at cars. Even then, $500 wasn't going to buy me a sporty little coupe or some muscle car like the Pontiac GTO I had envisioned. Dad did some checking, with his used car dealer clients, of course, and found the perfect car for his 16 year old son. It was a 1964 Ford Galaxy. It was white, built like a shoebox and had four doors and an automatic transmission. My girlfriend called it the "egg carton." It wasn't sexy, but it was only $400, ran like a top, and it was MINE.

Purpose

I had $100 left for gas and maintenance and Dad offered to insure it for a year and promised that we would talk about me picking up the insurance the following summer. I couldn't wait to drive myself to football practice the following week.

Over the school year, my extra funds ran out, I ran out of gas more than once, and my first car started to look more and more like the egg carton. I had wanted it *so* badly. But, the reality of owning it, being responsible for it, and paying for it loomed larger and larger with each passing day. I think Dad knew where this would all end up.

He had watched me set a goal, work for it and get there. He had helped me, both directly and subtly, knowing that sometimes you should be careful what you wish for.

I ended up selling that car the following spring and waited several years to buy another one. And, when I did, Dad was there to help me again. This time, I was better prepared, better financed, and much more aware of the responsibilities that sometimes come with getting what you want. By the way, that second car is still on my list of favorite cars I have ever owned. It was a 1968 Pontiac Lemans with a Hurst 4 speed transmission, and a 350 cubic inch engine – a true muscle car. I still miss it.

Purpose

Setting goals, sticking with them, and being responsible for the results are good lessons at any age. I was fortunate enough to learn them early.

Tip: Make setting goals a regular practice. Break them down into categories such as physical, financial, spiritual, family, social, and professional goals. Look at them each week as you plan your week, and align your activities to help you reach your goals.

Finally, take responsibility for getting there or not. It's all up to you.

Purpose

Chapter 2

PREPARATION

"The time to prepare isn't after you've been given the opportunity. It's long before that opportunity arises. Once the opportunity arises, it's too late to prepare." – John Wooden

Preparation

What Did You Learn Today -

As Dad believed that good luck was the result of being prepared to take advantage of our opportunities, we were constantly preparing. For what, we weren't sure. We just knew that life was supposed to be a continuous learning process. We were pretty good students and didn't take a lot of prodding to do our homework, but we were constantly reminded of our responsibility to learn something each and every day.

My father would come home from work every day, usually around 6:00 or so. He would walk into the house in his coat and tie and walk back to the bedroom to change into more comfortable clothes. Usually, unless we had done something wrong which was often handled by my mother with "just wait until your father gets home," we followed him into the bedroom. We couldn't wait to see Dad, talk to him, and hear what he had to say. Maybe that was because he rarely had much to say.

My father always started a conversation with a question. I suppose that it meant he didn't have to say what he was thinking, but he always started with a question. In later years, after we were grown, married, and gone, he would always start our telephone conversations with either "so, how's the car?" or "how's the dog?"

Preparation

In our childhood years though, without exception, he would always ask, "what did you learn today?" It didn't really matter whether it was something from school, from the playground, from sports, or from the neighborhood. And maybe it *was* just a conversation starter. We were all almost too eager to answer. We became focused on needing to have that answer ready when Dad came home. We learned that we had better learn something *every* day. Most important we learned that it was fun to learn new things. Dad created, or at least trained, our natural curiosity.

In business and in life, preparation is critical. Once an opportunity presents itself, it is too late to prepare. Making a conscious effort to learn something new, each and every day, will go a long way toward preparing you for the opportunities you will find.

Tip: Start each day with the goal of learning something new. Meet someone for the first time, read the newspaper, search the internet, ask a question. At the end of each day, you will know something new that you didn't the day before. At the end of the weeks, months, and years, you will be prepared for whatever comes along.

Preparation

You Can't Read Everything, but You Can Try –

Another one of the very special "regular" people who taught me so many of life's lessons was my mother. Many of the things that I have come to know have come, both directly and indirectly, from her. Mom is a voracious reader. We were talking recently and she told me that she estimates that she has read at least one book a week, every week, since she was five years old. Because I learned from my Mom that you never ask a woman her age, or tell anyone else, I won't tell you how old she is. Let's just say she has read somewhere in the neighborhood of 4,500 books in her life. Is that every book? Not even close, but it's a lot of books.

Mom is a very smart lady in her own right. Her parents were both college graduates in a time when most people, especially women, didn't have the opportunity to attend college. Mom is also a college graduate having majored in journalism. While she was a great Mom, I've often thought that she missed her calling not working for a newspaper or magazine publisher. In addition to teaching us impeccable manners and proper English grammar, she instilled in us a love of reading.

Reading magazines and the newspaper is good. Reading books is critical. There is so much you can learn by reading books. Business books, historical fiction, non-fiction, philosophy, and "how-to" books are wonderful opportunities to learn from other

Preparation

people who have been there and done that. Mysteries and fantasies are entertaining. They will engage your imagination and stimulate your creative brain. Books will educate you and give you things beyond the weather to talk about with the people you meet. Most important, they will expand your mind.

As the advertising campaign said a few years ago, "the more you read, the more you know!" The basic lesson I learned from my Mom was that you can't read everything, but you can try. What I have learned from doing all that reading is immeasurable. Thanks Mom.

> **Tip**: Visit your local bookstore or library at least once a month. Pick up a book, any book, and take it home to read. If you don't like it, put it down and get another one. Learn to enjoy the process and read a new book at least once a month.

Preparation

Preparation

Never Put on Wet Underwear –

Most of us are probably familiar with the Boy Scouts of America motto, "Be Prepared." It was from both my Boy Scouts experience and Dad that I learned the corollary "Never Put on Wet Underwear."

I must have been about 13 years old and was a Tenderfoot in the Boy Scouts. We met in the basement of our church. Older brother Don was well on his way to being an Eagle Scout. I, of course, was smitten by the outdoor skills being taught, the older guys, and the prospect of being a real man. Those were heady times.

I had been to summer Boy Scout camp where I worked on merit badges in canoeing, which I passed on the first try, and cooking, which I flunked repeatedly as I couldn't seem to bake a potato in the coals of an open fire without burning it. Don was a good Scout, a good big brother, and a good teacher. I still think of him today anytime I exchange a knife, hatchet, or axe with someone. "Hold the blade in your hand, extend the handle to the receiver, and don't give up control of the knife until the receiver acknowledges his control by saying thank you." These were the lessons of Totin' Chip – responsibility, safety, respect, and graciousness. We were not allowed to carry a pocket knife until we had learned Totin' Chip – and I desperately wanted to carry a pocket knife!

Preparation

I was ecstatic when I heard that our spring break Scout trip would be a camping trip to Mammoth Cave in Kentucky. Dad was going, Don was going, and I was going. I was going to be running with the big dogs! What could be better? We loaded our gear into the car along with at least two other Scouts and headed south. We had our tents, sleeping bags, hiking boots, clothes, camp stoves, food and no small amount of excitement. Bring on the adventure. We were prepared.

When we arrived at Mammoth Cave we were directed to the primitive campsites and set up camp. There had to be about three dozen scouts and five or six adult leaders. We were in pairs for the most part, usually an older boy with a younger boy. I was quite honored to be Jeff Bolin's tent mate. A year younger than my brother, he too was a good Scout and a good teacher. We carefully selected our tent sites, built fires for cooking and settled in. Tomorrow was to be our first day of exploring the world's largest cave system. What we had not prepared for were the torrential rains we got that night.

Fortunately for me, Jeff had selected a tent site on reasonably high ground. We had even taken the time to dig a small trench around the tent to keep water from seeping in. But it wasn't enough. It rained so hard and so long that one of our fellow Scouts, who had not been so diligent in selecting his tent site, literally floated, asleep on his air mattress, out of his tent and 40 or 50 yards down the dirt road until his air mattress ran aground. He woke up both lost and soaking wet.

Jeff and I fared a little better. We still got some water in the tent. Our sleeping bags were relatively dry, having rested on air mattresses. Our packs, however, had been sitting on the floor of the tent and absorbed way too much water and dirt. Our clothes were soaked. We got up, hung up what we could to dry, and dressed for our cave exploration in wet underwear, wet socks, wet pants, and wet shirts. We were warm enough, but we were wet. Undaunted, we assembled our motley troop and trudged off toward the caves.

The more I walked, the more uncomfortable I got. I didn't want to sound like a whiney tenderfoot so I gutted it out as long as I could. When the chafed thighs and blistered feet got so bad I couldn't stand it, I decided to say something to my Dad. His response? "Never put on wet underwear, son." He went on to show a little more concern and, in fact, I was fine. The day brightened, the sun came out and the clothes we had hung out to dry back at camp did just that.

I have to think Dad had managed to keep his stuff dry. He must have learned something about wet undergarments playing college football or in the Navy. In his mind, this was an obvious lesson that even a 13 year old should know.

Preparation

I know now and have known since that day that being prepared isn't enough. We have to be prepared for both the expected and the unexpected. We have to learn to adjust. Most important, we should always have a dry pair of underwear available – just in case.

Tip: Be prepared. Think through both what you expect to happen and what could happen. What is the best possible outcome, the worst possible outcome, and the most likely outcome. Prepare for a range of outcomes and be ready to adjust to any eventuality. You'll be glad you thought it through in advance.

Preparation

Listen. You Might Learn Something –

I wouldn't characterize Dad as a quiet man. Nor
would I characterize Mom as a talker. Rather, I
would say that Dad rarely, if ever, shared his real
thoughts or opinions and Mom often did. Given our
parents, I find it interesting that all three of us boys
developed into exceptionally verbal people. Well,
truth be told, we were all noted class clowns.

For the most part, we all got away with it because we
were also good students. Like most cut-ups, some
things we said were funny and some things not even
close to being amusing. We were constantly trying
out our material on Mom and Dad, in class, with our
friends – pretty much everywhere. Effectively, we
were developing our characters to be "characters."

Dad must have had that wry streak in him, too. But
for him, it was very subdued. Caution was his
watchword in nearly every circumstance. That may
have come from being an only child with a mother
who had no apparent sense of humor. It may just
have been part of being in his generation. He wasn't
stern. He was, just, well, Dad.

As boys around the dinner table, Don would usually
lead off with some off hand remark. My twin brother,
Bob, and I would join in, each of us trying to be
funnier or more clever than the other. Mom would
laugh, delivering an encouragement she probably
would regret, and on we would go. Dad would sit

41

quietly, absorbing everything. He smiled a lot, but I
don't remember him laughing very often. It wasn't
that he was unhappy. Dad didn't share his feelings –
with anyone.

When things would start to get a little too bold and a
little out of hand, Dad would calmly remark, "I think
that's enough." Frowns emerged on Mom's face and
the faces of her three smart aleck boys. Silence would
ensue and then Dad would say, "You know boys, if
you listen, you might learn something."

If we groused about going to church, Dad would say,
"If you listen, you might learn something." In fact,
any time we showed little or no interest in a given
event, Dad's admonition was always the same. "If
you listen, you might learn something."

Taking advantage of our opportunities was the first
of Dad's intended lessons. Preparing ourselves for
whatever might come down the road was a close
second. He knew that you can't learn much by
talking. He knew he didn't have anywhere near all of
the answers. But he also knew that he might get
some of those answers by listening to other people
who might have them.

There was always a quiet awareness in Dad. Looking
for opportunities, observing, listening, and quietly
processing the information at hand would serve him
well. It was a lesson he knew that we needed to
learn.

Preparation

Preparation

I never asked Dad what his core values were and if I had, I suspect he would have dodged the question. I know he had them. He just wasn't likely to share what they were.

If asked, this is what I think he would have said:
- Be observant
- Learn all you can
- Be gracious in every situation
- Be honest and loyal
- Work your tail off

They are all good lessons, to be sure. There are so many more, many of which you will learn as you read this book. Take what you like and make it yours. Please.

Tip: Take some time and develop your own set of core values. What is most important to you? What will you stand for? What will you not stand for? Write them down. It is important both for you and the people you serve to know your core values.

Preparation

Your Fly is Open –

Almost without fail, anytime I start to feel proud or smug, fate, Karma, or God steps in and lets me know that I'm just not that big of a deal. Some life force reminds me to laugh at myself.

Dad wasn't one to tell a joke, but he had a clever wit. His manner was usually deadpan but he was still funny. I walked into Mom and Dad's fourth floor condominium and saw him sitting in his chair reading the paper. I asked, "Where's Mom?" Without looking up from the newspaper, he said, "well, she's either in the bathroom or she jumped out the window!" Apparently, those were the only two options.

Years ago, I had done reasonably well as an insurance agent in a small town in Indiana. I decided to dress in my best khaki suit and drive to Indianapolis to call on some of the big boys. I arranged to meet with a childhood friend who had agreed to introduce me to some of the players in businesses in Indianapolis. After a brief introduction to several gentlemen seated in a conference room, one of the guys I was trying so hard to impress asked my friend and me if we were good friends. We looked at each other and said yes. He then asked if we were *really* good friends. Again, we looked at each other and said yes. He then looked at me and said, "good, then you won't mind me telling you that your fly is open."

45

Preparation

It was a humbling moment, but I had to laugh. What else could I do? Here I was, traveling to the big city with the sole purpose of impressing some of the heavy hitters and I was doing it with my zipper down! I've never forgotten that lesson. Laughing at yourself helps to keep you humble.

Over the years, I've been told that I am a funny person, although my wife probably doesn't think I'm funny anymore. There are too many reruns of the same old stories, I suppose. Humor is such a positive force in the universe. It can help to decompress a pressure situation. It can literally change the recipe for the chemical soup that runs through our bodies making us both healthier and happier.

Humor is about being able to laugh at yourself and your circumstances. Even in the worst of times, looking at life through the lens of a situation comedy can lighten our load. The important thing is that humor is not about making fun of anyone else. It is not about laughing at people. It's about laughing with people and the best object of that humor is yourself.

Tip: Take your Purpose seriously. Take Preparing for the opportunities to make a difference in someone's life seriously. Take surrounding yourself with quality People seriously. Take living by your values and setting your Priorities seriously. Take being Persistent seriously. But DO NOT take yourself or your circumstances too seriously. Laugh at yourself and with others. It's good for your soul.

Chapter 3

PEOPLE

"The next best thing to being wise oneself is to live in a circle of those who are." – C.S. Lewis

People

Friends Come and Go – Family is Forever –

My father always said that "friends come and go, but family is forever." In my experience over the years, I think that's true, but backwards. I think that we can define those people in our lives that come and go as friends, and those that stick with us through thick and thin as family. It really has nothing to do with biology or genetics. Heck, there's a college classmate of mine who is as much of a brother to me as my own twin. Why? Because we have been there for each other. We have shared happy times and sorrows. We have fought on a few occasions and disagreed on others. We have laughed. Oh my, how we have laughed. But I chose to be friends with him and he chose to be friends with me. We may not be related by birth, but we are definitely family.

At a recent college reunion, I had the chance to reconnect with over 100 of the men with whom I shared the college experience. It was an honor to be among them. Some were quite successful in business and some not. Some were in wonderfully happy marriages, and some not. Some were admirably healthy, and some not. It was an honor to be among them because we are brothers, not of the genetic sort but of the fraternal sort. There were no judgments, just understanding, fairness, and support. We had fun, drank a beer or two, laughed, and told all of the old stories (think of the movie, "Animal House"). It truly was an honor to be among these men both all those years ago and now.

51

People

I believe that associating with others breeds a kind of honor from that association. We have something in common, a shared experience. My years in college, my years in the fraternity, my years in the military, even my years on the high school football team, have built bonds with the other men in those groups that I will cherish for the rest of my life.

In most cases we get to choose the people with whom we will spend most of our time and who will potentially become part of our family, just as I chose the men I would live with in college.

Making good choices about people is not as easy as it might seem. How do we make good choices in terms of the people with whom we want to associate? In simple terms, I suppose that my mother was right. Believe only half of what you read and less of what you hear. One of my favorite holidays is Halloween, where many of us take great pleasure in masquerading as something or somebody we are not. The challenge in our lives is to figure out who is the real deal and who is in "costume."

In his book, *Mere Christianity*, C.S. Lewis tells us that there are two kinds of pretending. There is the bad kind, where pretense is there instead of the real thing; as when a man pretends he is going to help you but ends up stabbing you in the back. The second is a good kind of pretending, where the pretense leads up to the real thing. Very often the only way to acquire a quality in reality is to start behaving as if you already had it. If you are not feeling particularly friendly or happy, pretending as though you are starts to change your attitude and you literally become happier or more friendly.

This is why children's games are so important. Children are always pretending to be grown-ups, playing fireman, bulldozer driver, or doctor. All the time, they are hardening their muscles and sharpening their wits so that the pretending to be an adult helps them to grow up for real.

But, how do you know? How can we recognize those who are pretending for good and those who are pretending for evil?

While some people have become reasonably good at controlling their actions, they have no direct control over their fundamental temperament. One very telling example is to watch how someone treats the wait staff in a restaurant or the people who work at the local grocery store or recycling center. If that person is demeaning, arrogant, or simply mean toward the servers, chances are pretty good that their fundamental character includes these traits – no matter how they seem to be treating you. It's more probable that they want something from you and are acting civilized just long enough to get it. Simply said, what we are matters even more than what we pretend to do.

People

We choose our work place. We choose our friends. We choose our church, or our softball team, or our favorite hobbies based on the people we meet. Your priorities, your loyalties, lie with those whom you consider to be your family. While that can be, and hopefully includes, your biological family, it most certainly can include people from your company, former classmates, people from your neighborhood, or people from your church. The important thing is to choose those people wisely, because what we are is very often directly impacted by those people we choose as our "family."

> **Tip:** To get a quick gauge on a person, watch how they treat other people – especially those who are "serving" them. If they are not kind to the people from whom they cannot gain anything significant, find someone else to be part of your "family."

People

Be a Regular Guy -

Be a regular guy or gal. It's not easy. The better you get at whatever it is you do, the more you are tempted to let pride take over. As they say, "pride goeth before the fall."

When I was growing up, Dad never said much about his childhood, his college days, or his early adult life. In fact, he never talked about my grandfather either. I never really knew if he was just the strong silent type or was the product of a truly unremarkable life. Even in his late 80's, he would deflect any questions about his accomplishments with a sort of "aw shucks" attitude.

As a first generation American and the only son of two Scots, he was, at once, reserved, quiet, frugal (ok, he was tight with a buck), humble, and fun loving. Unfortunately for me, the only gene I seemed to get was the fun loving part.

When I was a kid, I knew that Dad had played a little football. Since I loved the game, I asked him about his football "career." And this is the story he told.

> I played a little in high school and really wanted to play in college. I wasn't big enough or fast enough and figured that I needed another year to mature so that I could compete. I knew my parents didn't have

enough money to send me to prep school for a year, so I decided to try and flunk out of high school. I thought they'd send me back through for another year, I'd get bigger and stronger, and off I'd go to college to play football. I wasn't all that bright, you know.

Well, mid-term grades came out and I was doing great with my plan – pretty much straight F's. My Dad took one look at those grades and let me know in no uncertain terms, that if I flunked out of high school, I would not be going back. He had a "wonderful" spot in his dry cleaning plant for me and I would be spending the rest of my life in that job.

I don't know that you've ever seen a kid work as hard to get his grades up from straight F's to passing in the second half of his final semester. I worked my tail off. And when it was all said and done, I passed my courses and graduated.

Your Grandpa, knowing what I really wanted, made arrangements for me to go to Germantown Academy for a year before going off to college. I got bigger, stronger, and faster and was able to play a little ball in college. I guess I grew up a little, too.

Dad went on to "play a little ball" at Ursinus, a small liberal arts school outside of Philadelphia. For him, that was the story. All of it. I found out the rest of the story from Mom. What he never mentioned was that he was the center on the varsity team, Captain of the team, and at one time was the leading scorer – as a center! He was THE star.

Ursinus is a small school and certainly no Notre Dame. But for me, it might as well have been Notre Dame. My Dad was a STAR football player. Picture a ten year old kid, selling programs at the Purdue – Notre Dame football game, proudly adorned in his Dad's burgundy letter sweater with a big "U" sewn on the front. People would ask what the "U" stood for. I knew they had no idea what or where Ursinus was, so I would just say "Urdue.' They would laugh, buy a program, and head toward Ross-Ade Stadium. I would watch them head off, knowing that *my* Dad was a star – and a humble one at that.

For him, he was just a regular guy.

More often that I care to admit, I need lessons and reminders in humility. I need only to think of Dad, a star by any measure, who knew that he was just a regular guy.

Ogden Nash, that great poet and humorist said it best:
> Sometime when you're feeling important,
> Sometime when your ego's in bloom.
> Sometime when you take it for granted,
> You're the best qualified in the room.

People

Sometime when you feel that your going
Would leave an unfillable hole,
Just follow this simple instruction
And see how it humbles your soul.

Take a bucket and fill it with water;
Put your hand in it up to the wrist.
Pull it out, and the hole that's remaining,
Is the measure of how you'll be missed.

You may splash all you please as you enter;
You may stir up the water galore;
But stop, and you'll find in a minute,
That it looks quite the same as before.

The moral in this quaint example
Is to do just the best that you can.
Be proud of yourself but remember,
There is no indispensable man!

                              -   Ogden Nash

Tip: Find someone you admire - someone
who is both talented and humble. There are
plenty of them out there, and yet certainly
not enough of them. Mirror their behavior.
Know that humility is a big part of your
path to Success.

People

We Don't Go To Sears -

Growing up in a small Midwestern town in the 1950's had a charm all its own. Sure we never went to a professional baseball game. We rarely, if ever, went to museums, stage productions, or big time circuses – or anything else that happened in the big cities one or two hours away. What we did do, was everything that Purdue University had to offer. I went to my first football game at the age of six and started selling Cokes, hot dogs, or programs at the age of eight. My best friend and next door neighbor's Dad was an assistant coach. At about ten years old, we were scalping our first tickets.

I learned to swim in the Purdue Fieldhouse pool, under the instruction of Hall of Fame coach Dick "Pappy" Pappenguth. Every Tuesday and Thursday evening during the winter, Dad or Mom would load us up in the car, take us down to the fieldhouse and drop us off for the swim team. I HATED those nights. Sometimes I would hide in the showers until the assistant instructors, all Purdue swimmers, would come in searching for me. Sure enough, they would drag my little rear end out to the pool and work me like a recalcitrant hunting dog. The session would finish, never too soon, and we'd head to the showers and march dutifully to Dad's waiting car, wet hair freezing in the frigid Indiana night air.

Every so often, the swim class would stage a competitive swim meet. Mom would come to watch

and cheer and applaud so hard for her boys that her hands would swell from the exploded blood vessels. Moms are great that way. No matter how you do, they think you are the greatest. And our Mom was no different.

We went to Purdue basketball games, baseball games, music recitals, and stage shows. Many of my friends' parents taught or worked at Purdue. I was, and am, a life-long, loyal Purdue fan. As such, I root for the Boilermakers in almost any contest, have a life-long distaste for both Notre Dame and Indiana University, and bleed Purdue Black and Gold.

But loyalty was even bigger in our house than colleges and sports teams. As a salesman for a small insurance agency in a small town, my Dad knew everyone. He knew his customers, and he knew those who weren't his customers. He knew his competition, and he knew who their customers were. We also knew those boundaries. No matter how popular a restaurant might be, if "we" didn't have it insured, we didn't eat there.

Two of the most popular restaurants in West Lafayette were, and still are, the Triple XXX and Bruno's. Triple XXX is a diner opened in 1929 (long before the movie rating system coined the term) near the university campus that has continued to serve hamburgers, root beer, and shakes to local residents even as the chain restaurants have come and gone. It holds the distinction of being the first and oldest

drive-in restaurant in Indiana. It's quite a place –
and we didn't go there. In those years, the owners
chose to buy their insurance from one of Dad's
competitors, so we chose to eat somewhere else. We
complained and Dad would explain the virtue of
loyalty to us.

Bruno's was an Italian restaurant, less than a block
from Triple XXX. Bruno was one of Dad's clients
from the first day they opened in 1955. We went to
Bruno's over and over again and can still claim his
children as friends. We learned to be loyal from Dad.

The first family cars I remember were Chrysler
products because that was the only dealership my
Dad had as a client. The local Dodge dealer finally
got a Fiat franchise and Dad immediately bought a
Fiat Spider convertible. Thankfully, a few years
later, Dad picked up the local Oldsmobile dealer and
we expanded our family vehicle choices.

In those days, there were only a couple of major
retail stores in Lafayette, J.C. Penney's and Sears.
Since Penney's was a national chain, and the only
one to supply Boy Scout uniforms, Penney's was
deemed to be an acceptable place to shop, even
though they weren't a client of my Dad's. Sears, on
the other hand, owned the Allstate Insurance
Company and sold insurance out of their store. They
competed directly with Dad and his firm. I can
honestly say that I didn't set foot in a Sears store

until I was 18 years old and away at school. In our house, we didn't shop at Sears!

To this day, I both understand and appreciate my father's dedication to his customers. He was one of the most loyal people I've known. It's one of the elements of the Boy Scout motto. It's a virtue by most any measure. It's something we live every day.

I have nothing against chain stores, chain restaurants, and global corporations. I just choose to do business with people like me and my Dad – simple guys in small towns who work and live with people they know.

> **Tip:** "It is not book learning young men need, nor instruction about this and that, but a stiffening of the vertebrae which will cause them to be loyal." – Elbert Hubbard
>
> It takes backbone to be loyal, but it is invariably worth the effort.

People

It Takes a lot of People to Make Up 7,000,000,000 (that's billion!) –

This is another one of those lessons that I did not learn from my father. In the category of learning something every day, I heard this from a business partner several years ago. I'm sure I was complaining at the time about someone who just didn't seem to think like I did. Have you ever heard yourself say, "what was he *thinking*?" I know I have. The fact is that other people don't think like you do because they are different than you are. And there are a lot of them!

There are almost seven billion people in the world today. It takes a lot of people to make up seven billion. Let me put it in perspective for you. If each and every one of us stood, arms outstretched, finger tip to finger tip, at the equator, we would circle the globe over 30 times! Put another way, there are between 10 billion and 80 *billion* galaxies in the observable universe and we are on but one planet in one solar system in one galaxy. Given those numbers, how significant do you feel? And every single one of those seven billion people is different. They have different genetic make-ups, different experiences, different perspectives. They want different things, have different motives, believe differently, think, perceive, and understand differently. That is why you find yourself saying "what was she *thinking*?"

People

People

No one is exactly like you. No one will encounter the same people you do. No one has the same opportunities each and every day that you do. And consequently, no one can have the same impact on earth as you can. That is what makes you, the choices you make, and your life, significant. While your significance is a result of your uniqueness, many of your frustrations are also a result of that uniqueness.

The first step is to understand that people are different. There are a number of studies of human personalities out there, but one of my favorites categorizes us into four basic groups.

The first group is the Lions. They are bottom line oriented and want action and quick results. They like to get things done. They love to be in charge, want feedback, and base their opinions on their view of reality. They live in the present. On the downside, they tend toward "ready, fire, aim," and think in the short term rather than the long term. They often lack trust in others and can tend toward the arrogant.

Our second group is made up of the Otters. Fun-loving and gregarious, these are the innovators and long range thinkers. They view the world as full of possibilities and solutions rather than problems. They live with an eye on the future. While their strengths include originality, imagination, and idealism, their weaknesses can be a scattered brain and deviousness.

The third group is the Golden Retrievers. They crave human interaction and are nurturers by nature. These are the people who love to be spontaneous and are both empathetic and persuasive. Their shortfalls may include impulsiveness, subjectivity, and the tendency to be manipulative. They tend to live in the past.

Our final group is the Beavers. These are the analytical thinkers. Their minds work with logic and analysis. They are well organized, deliberate, objective and rational. Unfortunately, they tend to be overly cautious and indecisive. They are often viewed as cold and unemotional or rigid. They tend to view time in the past, present, and future.

While there are many other systems of classification out there, each system groups people into some number of categories. The important things to remember are that you have a dominant style, may have tendencies in all of the groups, and are different than all of the other people you will encounter.

The second step is to embrace and appreciate those differences. Understanding how you think is important. More important is to understand how others think. This understanding will help you to appreciate and understand "what they were

thinking." Knowing that good teams require all
manner of skills, we can look to embrace those people
who have different personality skills than we do.

There are a lot of people out there. Your opportunity
to make a difference lies in your uniqueness.
Understanding that uniqueness, embracing it, and
using it to your advantage, is a key to your ultimate
success.

> **Tip:** Commit to learning more about
> personality styles, emotional intelligence,
> other people, cultures, and religions.
> Hundreds of excellent books and tapes are at
> your local bookstore, library, or online. Make
> it one of your goals for the coming year.

People

Oz Never Did Give Nothing to the Tin Man that He Didn't Already Have –

This line comes from a song released in 1974 by the band, America. I loved the song then and still do today. Not only was I already a huge fan of the whole Wizard of Oz concept, but I had already experienced it in real life.

I was 14 years old. I was about to enter high school as a freshman and Don was set to start his senior year. He and several of his friends from Boy Scouts cooked up a plan to hike a part of the Appalachian Trail. They planned to drive down to Gatlinburg, Tennessee, get a ride up to Davenport Gap, and walk some 60 miles or so to Mt. LeConte, where they would walk down and out of the woods to the car left behind. Their band of fellow scouts included three senior boys, one junior, and ME!

I couldn't believe it when Don asked if I would like to go along. It was the chance of a lifetime. Don, Dan, and Steve were the seniors and Greg was the junior. They each had some, or most, of the necessary gear. I, of course, had little or none. I had to get a suitable pack and pack frame, sleeping bag, canteen, pocket knife, boots, and clothes for the trip. I borrowed some, and Mom and Dad helped me buy what I couldn't find from friends. While I was assembling all of my personal belongings, the older boys were planning and assembling all of the group supplies.

The cook stove, dehydrated food, pots and pans, and first aid kit were included in that collection.

I'll never forget the meeting at Dan's house to split up the group supplies to add to our packs. It hadn't occurred to me that I would be carrying not only my own stuff, but my share of the group stuff, too. Everything was split into 5 piles, roughly equivalent in both weight and volume. I looked at my pile and my eyes must have looked like saucers. I remember thinking – I can't carry all of this stuff! Don looked at me and said "Don't worry Jim. You can do it. Besides, it'll be great conditioning for football this fall." I didn't know if any of that was true, but if Don said it, I was buying it. And, while I wasn't sure of it, I thought Don had had to do a pretty good sales job with the other guys to let his little brother go along. I wasn't about to disappoint him.

In the late 60's, camping gear wasn't anywhere near as sophisticated as it is today. Each of our packs weighed about 50 pounds. At that time, I was 5'10" tall and weighed 140 pounds. I knew I had a challenge in front of me. What I did not know, for sure, was whether I had what it took to meet that challenge. I had walked some of the streets around home with a loaded pack to get a feel for it, but there were no mountains, no rain, and no wet boots. There was a warm bed and real food to come home to. I was pretty sure I couldn't hack it. The most important single thing I had in my favor was the confidence and support of my older brother. That turned out to be all I needed.

About two days into the hike, my boots were soaked. Don suggested that I put them by the fire to help them dry overnight. What he neglected to mention was how close to the fire they should be. I woke up in the morning and retrieved my boots from the fireside, only to find that I had burned a hole in the toes of both boots. If they had been water resistant before, they certainly weren't now. The part of the boots that remained on the toe had become very stiff. Blisters were sure to come – and they did, in a big way. I was just going to have to tough it out. So I did.

There are few experiences in my life that I cherish more than that trip. We hiked. We talked about girls. We got wet. We got cold. We laughed. We strategized on how to get to the next planned shelter first so that we could claim five of the few available sheltered sleeping platforms for ourselves. We took great joy in out-hiking the Boy Scout troops and other groups that occasionally descended on the campsites. We awoke to bears pawing at our packs which were hanging inside the chain link fence that covered the open side of the shelters in bear country. We would turn in at night and the older boys would start pun contests. The puns were horrible and we laughed until we fell asleep. For me, it was as much joy as any 14 year old kid deserved.

For all the doubt, lack of physical preparation, and insecurity that goes with being a freshman in high school, I learned that I already had everything I needed. It was only a week, but we carried everything we needed to live. We had each other. And I had Don. As it turned out, Oz didn't need to give me anything that I didn't already have, either.

Tip: The song by America finishes with "So please, believe in me..." Believe in yourself. When you can't seem to do that, lean on your family and your friends - the people who believe in you. With their support and faith in your God, you will not fail.

Chapter 4

PRIORITIES

"It is not enough to be industrious, so are the ants. What are you industrious about?" – Henry David Thoreau

Priorities

Priorities

Tortoises and Hares –

In the Air Force, they call them "fast burners." These are guys who rise quickly through the ranks, typically starting as pilots, and often ending up as Colonels or even Generals. They all have talent. Many have native intelligence. Some have the heart, or drive to succeed. Those that succeed are typically an inspiration to the rest. They are the hares in the children's story, except that in the children's story, the hare loses the race to the tortoise.

The tortoise also has talent and native intelligence and drive. His best quality, however, is his ability to stick with his priorities. That dogged focus on his priorities is what sets him apart. In the children's story, of course, he wins the race. Dad and the great majority of his friends were tortoises. They weren't flashy. They didn't work for, and rise to the top of, big corporations like General Motors or Caterpillar or General Foods. They were entrepreneurs – independent businessmen. Like the tortoise, they had talent. They had intelligence. They had heart. But most of all, they had that dogged dedication to their priorities that ensured their success in business, in their families, in their communities, and in their lives.

I was 38 years old and had been working with Dad for almost 10 years. Not only had we become good friends, but I enjoyed the friendship of his friends and contemporaries as well. I felt as if I had earned

Priorities

their respect. One sunny Saturday, I found myself at the golf club with some of my buddies. We had played in the morning and were having lunch on the patio, overlooking the tenth tee. My Dad and his regular golf group walked onto the tee. By this time, I had taken off my golf shoes but walked out onto the tee to say hello in my flip-flops. There they were: Dad, Wes, Spider, and Byron, all contemporaries of my Dad and all with sons my age. Feeling a little surge of teenage-like testosterone around these old guys, I asked if I could use one of their drivers and hit a ball – in my flip-flops. Naturally, I intended to hit one very long and straight and impress my Dad and his companions.

Byron handed me his driver and I asked for a ball. Four hands were extended, each with a golf ball for me to hit. One was a range ball, the free ones they give you to hit in the practice area. Dad had a ball in his hand that had been in some pond so long that it had a brown ring around it rendering it a stunning small model of Saturn. Spider's ball had enough scuff marks from bounding along the cart paths that it could be used for sandpaper. Finally, Byron held out a Pink Lady. This ball was pink! Pink Ladies were very popular among the women and were very soft and known not to go very far. I couldn't believe it. Four men, all who had been very successful in business and had few financial limitations and they were playing with golf balls a high school kid wouldn't use.

Priorities

I looked at these four very successful men, a real estate agent, two insurance agents, and an independent manufacturers' representative. I was stupefied. I looked at the group and said "for God's sake, you all have more money than God. Can't you afford to buy a decent golf ball?" Almost as if rehearsed, they looked at each other, then at me and said, in unison, "Maybe, that's why we have more money than God!"

Not only was it a great lesson in humility, but it was a great lesson in priorities. For the first time in my life, I understood that in order to be successful in the long run, most of us have to make many small sacrifices along the way. Dad and his buddies were fond of saying that you have to have money to make money. One way to ensure that you have money when opportunities arise is to be frugal and judicious with what you have.

As Dad got older and retired to Florida, I would play golf with him on a beautiful layout along the intercoastal waterway. Almost every hole was bordered by water or had some sort of pond or creek running through it. Without fail, Dad would hit a shot, then walk along the water's edge with his ball retriever in hand, looking for all those lost golf balls the "hares" of the world had no time to retrieve. He always had a large shoebox in his trunk where he kept all those rescued balls. He had plenty to share with friends and grandkids. I don't know for sure, but I doubt he ever bought a new golf ball in his life.

Priorities

Here's to the tortoises of the world!

> **Tip:** Successful people, and most especially entrepreneurs, take risks, but only intelligent risks. They think through the alternatives, selecting the best. They are willing to make the small sacrifices necessary to move them toward their ultimate goal. Be willing to "play with old golf balls" with pride. Select your priorities carefully. You will end up winning the long race.

Priorities

Put It Back Where You Found It –

Another of my many fond childhood memories is puttering around in Dad's "shop." Now Dad was neither handy nor incapable. He was somewhere in between those descriptions. He built a small sailboat when we were very young, and finished off a part of our basement with a bar, barn siding on the block walls and faux brick tiles on the floor. In his view, the money he saved by doing it himself was much better spent on the pool table his boys so desperately wanted.

As the years went on, he also built a brick patio with a brick retaining wall/bench seat and the matching brick sidewalk around the house from the driveway to the back yard. It was a pretty impressive undertaking and all of us boys helped. The sailboat, the basement project, the patio project, the landscaping – none of them were things my Dad grew up doing. He just had to read a little bit about the "how to," talk to somebody who had done similar things before, and dive in. Among the lessons we learned by helping out were the importance of being willing to try new things, to make mistakes and learn as you go, and to use the right tools.

Dad's "shop" was a small room in the basement which also housed the furnace/air conditioning system. It wasn't much, but it was his territory. I'm pretty certain that Mom never set foot in that room. As his sons however, we had a sort of permissive use

pass. He wanted us to be comfortable trying new things and using his tools. There was just one simple rule – put it back where you found it!

I brought an old lawnmower engine home when I was about 14 and was sure I could get it running and use it as the foundation of a go-kart. I dismantled it on Dad's workbench. As I began to reassemble it, I had a number of parts left over. Needless to say, it never did run and pieces, parts and tools were scattered on the workbench for weeks, if not months.

A couple of years later, when my brothers and I had a rock band, we would constantly be fixing microphones, guitar cords and such with Dad's soldering gun and a little silver solder. Again, we tended to leave pieces and parts all over the workbench. I'm sure Dad was a little annoyed by the mess, but what really set him off was coming down to the workshop and not being able to find his stuff. All he asked was that we put it back where we found it.

All these years later, I realize that Dad encouraged us to experiment, to try new things, to fail, to learn. All of those things are important. But each of those lessons must be tempered with respect. He expected us to respect his shop, his territory. He expected us to respect his tools, his stuff. And he expected us to learn that respect for people's space and tools would lead to respect for those people.

Priorities

When it's all said and done, respect for others is all about being considerate – considering how what you are doing, saying, and thinking affects others. Respect is about understanding what others have to offer in the form of lessons, encouragement, advice, and wisdom. Respect is about leaving things better than you found them and, at the very least, putting the tools back where they belong.

Tip: The next time you borrow a tool from your friend or neighbor, make certain it goes back to them better than it was when you got it. Fill it with gas, wash it, sharpen it, whatever it takes. Not only are you demonstrating your respect for their stuff, you are demonstrating your respect for them. And, by the way, they'll be really happy to loan you their tools in the future.

Priorities

Walk, and Carry Your Own Clubs -

My father played golf a couple of times a week well into his 80's. In the last year or two he had to ride in a cart. It wasn't all that long before, barely more than five years in fact, that Dad walked the golf course almost every day, carrying his bag, and playing a very respectable round of golf.

About two years before he was forced by near blindness to quit the game, Dad's back gave out on him. After visiting several doctors, we met with an orthopedic/back specialist. In addition to an All-American smile, an engaging personality, and a natty wardrobe, the guy was reportedly a very good surgeon. He explained that "minor surgery" is surgery *someone else* is having. He added that a *haircut* would qualify as major surgery if a general anesthetic were necessary. Then he asked if Dad was "active." Dad, in his usual deadpan way, said that "for an old fat guy, I guess I'm pretty active." By the way, while he was arguably old, he was never fat. I told the doctor that, until his back gave out, Dad had been playing golf several times a week and until a couple of years before had walked and carried his own bag. This fine young doctor looked at my Dad and said, "I want to grow up to be you!"

Simply put, Dad had a passion for golf, for being outdoors, for being active, for people. In his view, and as that first generation son of Scottish immigrants, golf was a game to be played while walking. His

priorities were about getting some exercise, some fresh air, and some companionship. It was about a little healthy competition. There was no need for golf carts, or cart paths, or "trail" fees. The course should be walked, much as one would take a walk in the park.

Maybe that's why Dad played until he just couldn't. He appreciated the fundamental nature of the outdoor game. Whether he won or lost was really not that important, although he *always* competed. He simply focused on the fundamentals and let the results take care of themselves. Maybe we would all be better off to follow that lead. Be passionate about everything we do. Focus on the fundamentals of whatever that may be. Let the results simply be what they are and enjoy the walk in the park along the way.

Tip: Your fundamentals begin with your Purpose. Always think about your Purpose as you consider your Priorities for today, this week, this month, and this year.

Priorities

I Don't Have Time is a Lie -

I hear people say this over and over again, "I don't have time." The fact is that we all have the same number of hours in each day and we choose what to do with those hours. We choose whether to stay in bed, get up and go to exercise class, write a letter to our mothers, take out the trash, clean the garage or paint the house. We choose what kind of work we want to do, where we want to live, who we want to live with, what hobbies we like to engage ourselves in. Our lives are a collection of our choices.

Almost thirty years ago, my older brother, Don, was diagnosed with pseudo-masticular carcinoma. That's Cancer, with a capital C. Three years older than my twin brother and me, Don was like many older brothers and first-borns. He was perfect! Please understand that, all these years later, I still believe he was perfect. Mom believes he was perfect. Dad believed he was perfect. I suppose that Don was not really perfect, he just seemed like it. He was a good looking guy, a good athlete, had the lead in all the school plays, got great grades, and dated the best looking girls. He played the piano by ear and could sing just as well. He was funny, caring, and understanding. He wrote beautifully. I idolized him. Don played football, so I played football. Don acted in our high-school plays, so I acted (poorly, I might add) in our high-school plays. When he was a senior and I was a freshman, Don played the Scarecrow in the *Wizard of Oz*. I auditioned for, and got, a bit part as

a Winkie. For those of you who are not familiar with
the original stage version of the show, the Winkie
was modified slightly in the more famous movie to be
the wicked witch's tall green guards. These were
then augmented with the flying monkeys. Imagine a
freshman boy in high school, dressed entirely in
yellow (not green), including yellow tights, and
bounding around the stage like a crazed canary. You
get the picture. Don was a star. I was a bit player,
but willing to thoroughly embarrass myself to be
around him. I cannot remember a time in my life
that I laughed more and enjoyed myself more than in
the rehearsals and performances of that high school
production with Don. I can still do the better part of
each of his songs and lines. In my eyes, he WAS
perfect and I wanted to be just like him.

After one year of college, Don transferred from
Miami of Ohio to Indiana University to join his high
school sweetheart Lynne, who, not surprisingly,
played the part of Dorothy in the *Wizard of Oz*. A
year later, they were married, with only reluctant
approval from Mom and Dad, principally because
they were so young. They finished college. Don joined
the Navy as an Officer and followed his Navy stint
with law school. Everything was coming up roses for
my perfect big brother. Then, as in most lives, things
began to change.

Don and Lynne were growing up and, predictably,
growing apart. Divorce soon followed with no
children to complicate the issues. Mildly

Priorities

disheartened with his "failed" marriage, Don moved to Los Angeles, joining my twin brother, Bob, in the westward movement of the Bain family and started his career as an attorney. He was 29.

Around Christmas time, slightly more than a year into his new career and new life, Don discovered a small lump in his neck, right at the jaw line. Not wanting to spoil the holiday, he waited until shortly after New Year's Day to see a doctor. The doctor suggested that he keep an eye on it and scheduled an appointment three weeks later. By then, the lump was the size of a baseball. Surgery in late January was followed with radiation therapy. Those of us who were inclined to do so, prayed. The rest of the family crossed their fingers. In May, Don and Bob were standing in line waiting to order a hamburger at McDonalds. Bob looked at Don's neck and asked, "it's back, isn't it?" The cancer had come back. By now, we knew it was in his lymphatic system and the prospects were dire. He moved home to Indiana from California in June. Coincidentally, I completed my tour with the U.S. Air Force that same month and moved back to Indiana to start my career working with Dad in the insurance business. Don lived, if you call slowly dying living, with Mom and Dad. We all watched in complete helplessness and despair as his health and his will to fight waned. Over the summer, Don had several stays in the hospital, being admitted for the last time in late September. He passed away two weeks later. By that time, I had been working with Dad for barely four months. We would see each other at the office and I would ask Dad if he was going to go see Don in the hospital today. He would, more often than not, respond with, "I don't have time."

I was hurt, confused, disappointed and angry. Like many young men, I was pretty sure that, like Don, my Dad was also perfect. How could it be that he didn't have the time to go see his dying son! Dad was not in the room with Don the day he died, I was. After his death in October, Dad couldn't bring himself to view Don's body at the funeral home. I stepped up to handle the funeral details – Dad just couldn't. He couldn't even talk about Don. Now I'm no psychologist, but I do know that my father's response to this whole tragic situation was not emotionally healthy.

And there is the lesson. My Dad *did* have the time to see his dying son - my perfect brother. He had the time to work, to play golf, to eat, and to sleep. He *chose* not see him. Looking back, my father made those choices to protect himself against an unimaginable hurt. I now know that he chose not to see Don, not because he didn't want to, but because he couldn't. The important point is that he *chose*.

How we choose to spend our time is a direct reflection of our priorities. We cannot say we love to read, but never spend any time doing it. We cannot say we love our family and then choose to spend time with everyone and everything other than our family.

Priorities

We cannot say we would love to be in great physical shape and then spend our time on the couch in front of the television. Ben Franklin is credited with saying that "Time management is self management." Each of us must decide what our priorities will be for today, for this week, this month, this year, for our life. Then we must make the choice to spend time on those priorities. "I don't have time" is a lie! The truth is "I choose not to take the time." Choose wisely.

Tip: Eliminate "I don't have time" from your vocabulary. Start being honest with yourself about your priorities and say, "I choose not to make the time."

Priorities

Priorities

If You Don't Have Time to Do It Right –

"If you don't have time to do it right, what makes you think you have time to do it over?" I'm not sure exactly what my Dad was trying to teach me when he asked me this – over and over and over, again. I'm pretty certain that what he really wanted was a job well done, and one HE would not have to do over. But the question is really two-fold, isn't it?

The first question is about how we use our time, how we select which things to do from our long list of possibilities. Most of us have more things to do than we have time for. So, how do we choose? If Franklin was right in saying that "Time management is self management," then the first step in effective self management is establishing priorities in how we will spend our time. I know that most of us, including me, all too often talk a good game, but fail to deliver the promised results. We lament our physical condition – the weight we are carrying, the shape we are in, the exercise we should be getting – all from the comfort of the recliner. We cannot continue to claim that getting into shape is a good idea, and spend no time exercising, or even getting off of our lazy butts. We cannot raise the banner of family and spend no time with them. We cannot talk of the importance of spirituality in our lives and never go to church, meditate, or pray. All of those are shams. Our REAL priorities lie in the things on which we spend our time and ultimately our lives. So, taking a few minutes to align the time we have to spend with the things we think are important is the first step to self management and time management.

Here are some suggested categories to get you started:

I grew up in Indiana and while I was not raised on a farm, several of my friends were. I heard a lot about 4H, the agriculture community's answer to Boy Scouts and the YMCA. I learned, from my friends, that the 4 H's are Head, Heart, Health, and Hands. Those are a pretty good starting point for deciding what your priorities are. What are you doing today to help you improve or grow in your Head? What have you read, what have you learned, what do you know today that you didn't know yesterday? How will you grow in your Heart, today? Have you told those that are close to you that you love them? Have you spent a few moments thanking your God? How will you be Healthier today than you were yesterday? Have you eaten as you should? Have you exercised? And finally, have you spent any time today working with your Hands? On the farm, this can be taken very literally. But really, it's about work. Have you done a good day's work today? Have you made the world a little bit better place by your efforts? It's all about choices. How we spend our time screams volumes about what we believe is most important in our lives.

I'll make it even easier with two more examples. The YMCA uses a three part model for self management. Their model includes Mind, Body, and Spirit. Sound similar? It should. Again, we need only look at these three areas in our lives, decide what is important to us in each area, and begin to work each day to make ourselves better in each area. The formula is simple. The execution is not.

And finally, for those for whom simple is too simple, here is a model with eight categories and a simple quiz you can do right now to see where your priorities really lie.

Balanced Lifestyle Exercise

For each of the following statements enter in the numbered box the percentage (0-100) that best describes you.

For example: 1. I take time to listen – 30%

	1. 30	2.	3.	4.	5.	6.	7.	8.
	9.	10.	11.	12.	13.	14.	15.	16.
	17.	18.	19.	20.	21.	22.	23.	24.
Total								
Avg.								

Priorities

So let's begin:

1. I take time to listen to people
2. I spend time meditating/praying daily
3. I stick to an exercise routine six days a week
4. I spend sufficient time with my family
5. I have money that works for me and/or people who work for me
6. I am satisfied with my career
7. I still pursue new interests / activities
8. I read at least one book per month
9. I make friends easily
10. I have an intimate relationship with God
11. I eat a nutritious diet six days a week
12. I write or talk to all members of my family regularly
13. I have sufficient income to provide for my basic needs
14. I make a difference through the work I do
15. I have an exciting hobby which I pursue regularly
16. I attend seminars or other learning opportunities
17. I meet at least two new people per week
18. I attend spiritual gatherings or events regularly
19. I participate in some physical activity regularly
20. I enjoy regular family reunions, gatherings or outings
21. I have a detailed retirement investment plan

Priorities

22. I maintain a healthy balance between my personal and professional life
23. I contribute personal time for community projects
24. I often listen/watch audio/video recordings to learn more

	1.	2.	3.	4.	5.	6.	7.	8.
	9.	10.	11.	12.	13.	14.	15.	16.
	17.	18.	19.	20.	21.	22.	23.	24.
Total								
Avg.								

After reading the statements and completing the balanced living grid, total each column (add blocks #1, # 9, and # 17) and enter that number in the "Total" block. Then divide that number by 3 to get your Average.

Priorities

Example:
3. I stick to an exercise routine 6 days a week -
entered "60"

11. I eat a nutritious diet 6 days a week – entered
"70"

19. I participate in some physical activity regularly –
entered "80"

60 + 70 + 80 = 210
210/3 = 70, so Physical areas of your life = 70%

You have now rated the major areas of your life. For
example, statements #1, #9, and #17 relate to your
social life. Numbers 3, 11 and 19 cover the physical
areas of your life. The areas are:

- Social (1, 9, 17)
- Spiritual (2, 10, 18)
- Physical (3, 11, 19)
- Family (4, 12, 20)
- Finance (5, 13, 21)
- Professional (6, 14, 22)
- Recreational (7, 15, 23)
- Intellectual (8, 16, 24)

Plot your average for each category on the chart and
connect the dots with a rough shape. The more your

shape looks like a perfect circle, the more balanced your life is.

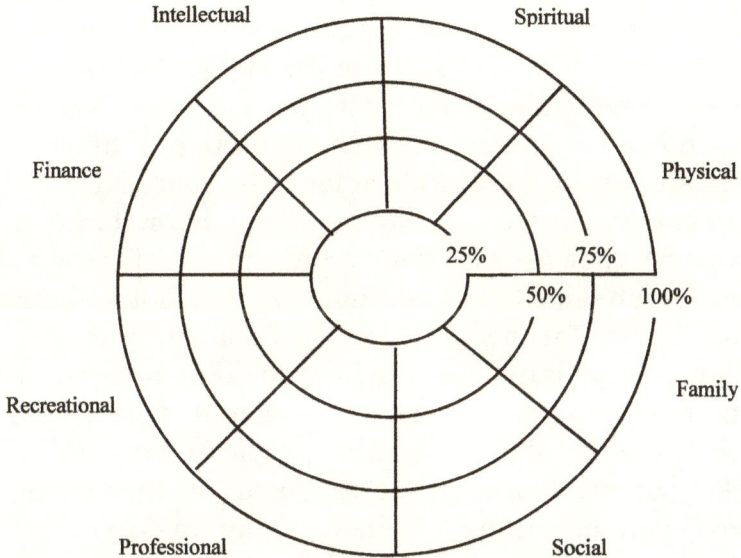

Here are a couple of questions you might ask yourself.

- In which areas did you score the highest?
- Are there areas where you would like to invest more time?
- What aspects of your lifestyle are you aware of that complicate your life?
- What impact do these aspects have on your performance, health and relationships?

Priorities

Once we have established our priorities, we can focus our efforts on those things that are important to US.

Again, my Dad's question: "If you don't have time to do it right, what makes you think you have time to do it over?" If the first part of that lesson is time management, the second is pride. The area we grew up in had a significant Amish population. While the Amish are often best known for their beards (the males), conservative dress, and disdain for things modern, they are also known far and wide for their craftsmanship. They are a hard working lot and are well known for the quality of the furniture they make. Very simply, they believe in doing it right, in their case, for God's sake. The long and short is that while the Amish are a humble people and are not as likely to put their name on the furniture they make, we should be willing to sign anything we do. Our signature says that we have done the best we can and are proud of the work. The work represents our very best and anyone who uses or benefits from our work should know that we have done our very best on their behalf. Remember, it's not about you – it's about them. Do it right the first time!

Priorities

Tip: Whether you choose the 4H model, the YMCA model or the Balanced Lifestyle model, it is important to balance your life. Evaluate on a regular basis where you are in the important areas of your life. Then *change* whatever you need to in order to bring your life back into balance. Balance and priorities are about how you *choose* to spend your time.

Priorities

Chapter 5

PERSISTENCE

"Nothing in the world can take the place of persistence. Talent will not; nothing is more common than unsuccessful men with talent. Genius will not; unrewarded genius is almost a proverb. Education will not; the world is full of educated derelicts. Persistence and determination alone are omnipotent" – Calvin Coolidge

If You're Looking for Sympathy –

We grew up in a "tough love" house. I don't ever remember being spanked although I'm sure I probably was. I do remember "the belt," which was in the kitchen cupboard, right near the door, presumably for easy access. Again, I don't ever remember Dad using that belt for what we firmly believed was its intended purpose, but by golly, we KNEW it was there.

We were expected to behave, both at home and when out in public, and we were punished in one form or another when we didn't. I remember one day, sitting at the piano. I couldn't play anything in spite of Mom's best intentions. Some classic sweet matronly type came over to the house to give us lessons, which as young boys, we took to like cats take to a bath. Don was interested and showed some promise, but Bob and I were not so hot.

So I was sitting at the piano just banging on the keys. Dad was obviously annoyed. After several increasingly unpleasant and unsuccessful requests for me to stop, he reached his limit and gave me a "love tap." Love taps usually came to the side of the head and were swift and sure. I got the message. Unfortunately for Dad, I woke up the next day with a very coincidental case of pneumonia including a high fever, nausea, and a headache. Mom, of course, thought Dad had killed me with his "love tap." I'm pretty sure I never got slapped again after that.

Persistence

Persistence

As I grew older I heard someone say, "if you're looking for sympathy, you'll find it between "shit" and "syphilis" in the dictionary." It's a concept my Dad instilled in us without ever speaking the words. It wasn't that Dad didn't love us completely. Quite the opposite. He had learned the lessons of "tough love" from his parents and he intended for us to learn those lessons, too.

We learned early on to tough it out, lick our wounds and move on. Feeling sorry for ourselves, or expecting anyone else to feel sorry for us was simply not an option. My Dad learned it from his father. He taught us, and I taught my boys. Just when you start to think you have everything figured out and things are going well, here comes the bad bounce of the ball. If you're lucky, you'll catch the ball. More probably, you'll make your best effort, but miss. And sometimes, you'll get hit square in the jaw by the ball. Either way, you can't spend any time expecting anyone to feel sorry for you. The next ball will be coming all too soon.

Get up, dust yourself off, and get ready for the next one. It's coming and you had better be prepared.

Persistence

> **Tip:** Whenever you have a bad moment, or even a series of tough times, remember this line from a sign in our high school baseball locker room. It said "a bad bounce is no excuse – anybody can catch the good ones."

Persistence

What is the Best I Can Do from Here? –

One of the most critical elements of Persistence is
the ability to get past your mistakes – and those of
the people around you. Professional level athletes
know this. A baseball pitcher has to forget about the
home run ball he just threw and pitch to the next
batter. The football quarterback needs to forget
about the interception he just threw, and go back out
and drive his team down the field. The golfer needs
to forget about the shot he just hit into the woods
and figure out "what is the best I can do from here?"

I think most of us are a little scared of our Dads
when we're growing up. Maybe it's because Mom
always said things like "just wait until your Dad gets
home!" At least in our case, Dad tended to be pretty
hard on himself when he made a mistake and we
assumed he would be equally unforgiving of us. That
perception changed dramatically when I was about
17.

Dad was always a "car guy." He didn't tinker with
old cars or anything like that, he just liked his cars.
Because he had a Chrysler dealer as a client, we
nearly always had Dodges or Chryslers as our family
car. Dad was in his 40's when the local Chrysler
dealer struck a deal to also sell Fiats. I'll never forget
it. We were all old enough to drive, Dad didn't need a
car with a back seat to haul us around and my older
brother had a used Dodge Dart that the boys were
expected to use. If more than one of us needed a car,

Persistence

Mom's Chrysler Newport was available. So Dad bought a Fiat 124 Spider Coupe – his first toy. It was a canary yellow, two door sports car with a stick shift and a black convertible top. Call it a mid-life crisis if you like, but I think he just wanted something he could call his.

He'd had it about six weeks and although he would deny it, I think he may have slept in the garage with his new car on a couple of occasions. He was truly smitten with his new ride. That's when he and Mom decided to travel to Illinois with some friends for an away Purdue football game. They left early on Saturday morning in Mom's car and weren't expected back until late that night. His instructions were both brief and straightforward. "Don't drive the Fiat!" We had Don's old Dodge Dart to drive if we needed it so I think he felt pretty comfortable that his car was safe.

I couldn't resist the temptation to jump into that beautiful sports car, take the top down, and cruise around town. I'd see my buddies and with any luck, pick up a girl and take her for a ride. I'd only been out about 30 minutes when disaster struck. A gentleman in his 80's completely missed a yield sign and creamed the left front side of Dad's new car! Now the accident wasn't my fault, but I was pretty certain that fact was going to be completely irrelevant.

I spent the afternoon on the phone with every body shop in town, asking if they could fix the car THAT

Persistence

DAY. It was a ridiculous question and I knew it, but I had no choice. With no luck to be had, I simply had to wait for Dad to get home and explain, as best I could, what had happened. Dad was really angry, but he didn't explode. In fact, I don't know that I ever saw him explode over anything, but if he were going to, this would have been it. He was disappointed in me. He was angry. He was eerily quiet.

I know I didn't sleep much that night and Sunday seemed to be one of the longest days of my life. It's the only day I ever recall that Dad would not, or could not, speak to me. Sunday evening came and I just didn't know what to do. I took my driver's license out of my wallet, walked into his den and handed it to him. I said, "I'm sorry Dad. I made a mistake. I shouldn't have taken the Fiat and I shouldn't have ignored your one request. Here's my license. Keep it as long as you want and give it back to me when you think I'm ready for the responsibility of having it."

He took it, paused for a minute and handed it back to me. He said, "I think you've already learned your lesson. We all make mistakes. The question is what will you do from here?"

Persistence is tough. You have to get up every day and keep going in the face of disappointments and mistakes. Until you learn that we all make mistakes and that we need to forgive ourselves, learn from them, and move on, Persistence is nearly impossible.

Tip: When you make a mistake, remember these tips:

1. You're human. Get over it. Forgive yourself.
2. Be remorseful. You may well have hurt others by your mistake. You will want to let them know you are sorry.
3. Learn the lesson. Move on. Make yourself a better person as a result, today, tomorrow, and for the rest of your life.

Persistence

"Try? There is no try. There is only do."

Or, if all else fails, get a bigger hammer.

So, by now, hopefully, you've given some thought to your Purpose. You have learned how to Prepare yourself for any opportunity that may come your way. You've learned about choosing good People with whom to surround yourself. You may have already considered your Priorities based on your Purpose. You have worked hard. Now you must be Persistent at whatever it is you do. Based on our model, you will have Success in your life.

But it doesn't always work that way, does it? Sometimes, no matter what we do, things go wrong, sometimes horribly wrong. There are no guarantees. We can only keep focusing on the P's, the fundamentals, and letting the results take care of themselves.

I was shocked a few months ago to learn that the movie "Star Wars" was released over 30 years ago. I've never been a big sci-fi fan, but I loved this series of films. The model is classic. Good against evil. Over-matched underdogs victorious against all of the odds. It was a true "feel good" film, and fun to watch.

Of all the movie lines I remember, one that stands out above the rest is the great teacher Yoda, passing on the wisdom and skills of the Jedi Knights to young Luke Skywalker, the ultimate good guy and

Persistence

hero. During the scene, Yoda is watching Luke practice his light sabre skills. And try as he might, he can't seem to master the use of this weapon. Yoda admonishes Luke, who responds with exasperation, saying "I'm trying!" Yoda seizes the teaching moment, and says, "Try? There is no try. There is only do."

When things aren't going well, we have to quit "trying" and trust our instincts, our skills, our fundamentals. We must trust our Purpose, our Preparation, our People, and our Priorities. We need to BELIEVE that we can do whatever it is we are doing. There is no room for doubt. We must have the confidence that we are doing the right things and that if we continue to do the right things, good results will happen.

Sounds simple, doesn't it. But it's not. It takes practice. Confidence is a matter of doing something over and over again, until you no longer have to try - you only have to do. Think about this for a minute. I have played golf with an accomplished neurosurgeon. This is a man who routinely operates on people's brains! He is skilled and confident. He knows his work and has become markedly proficient at it. He has done it over and over and over again.

But you should see this guy try to make a three foot putt! He lacks the confidence in his golf game that he has in brain surgery. He's *trying* to make the putt rather than trusting his instincts and skills and just doing it. Which of these activities has a bigger penalty for failure? Obviously, brain surgery. And yet, our intrepid weekend golfer struggles with a three foot putt. I suspect that had he spent as much time practicing his putting as he does in brain surgery, he wouldn't miss very often.

My Dad used to say it this way. "When all else fails, get a bigger hammer." In other words, find a way to give yourself the confidence you need to quit *trying* and just *do*.

Focus on Purpose, Preparation, People, Priorities, and Persistence, and Success will come. Trust me. More important, trust yourself.

Tip: "Whether you think you can or you think you can't - you're right." – Henry Ford

Always be confident in your abilities and positive about your choices. It will pay huge dividends.

Persistence

Be the Person Your Dog Thinks You Are -

Not long ago we had a very somber day in our house. Our German Shepherd, Kiesha, passed late one night. She was thirteen and had been diagnosed two weeks before with lung cancer. I suppose that is the one downside to having a pet for its entire life. They become such a big part of *your* life. She was the matriarch of our in-house pets. Our Golden Retriever and our cat were both wandering the house looking for the boss. They knew that the house just wasn't in order. Something wasn't right.

Now, we are not naïve enough to think that we are the first or the only people to grieve over the loss of a pet. And we have experienced the much more devastating loss of people in our family. But that didn't make this loss any easier. It was still a loss and it still hurt.

We learned a lot from Kiesha. She was classically loyal and very protective. She was wonderfully kind, even to our one year old cat with whom she loved to play. She never stopped running, exploring, and enjoying her world. She was lean, strong, and brave. She was both loving and loved. She was a nearly perfect companion.

I won't forget how she would dig up our bushes, go nuts during thunderstorms tearing up anything and everything to get away from the thunder, and how she would cower if you looked at her cross-eyed. But

119

Persistence

Persistence

I will remember those traits, not as flaws, but as what made her unique – and real.

If we want to learn some lessons about how life should be lived, we need only look to our dogs. They don't complain. They just keep being who they are. And they, for reasons I don't fully understand, love us unconditionally. Her shortcomings with us pale in comparison to our mistakes with her. And yet, to the last, she loved us. As I lament her passing, I'm reminded of that great line that I heard delivered by Norman Schwarzkopf, who said, "Just be the person your dog thinks you are!" Great advice. I can only try to measure up.

> **Tip:** Being the person your dog thinks you are requires that you know the unlimited nature of your capabilities. Set your goals high – and reach for them.

The Sun Don't Shine on the Same Dog's Ass Forever! –

The fact is that life has its ups and downs. We learned that from my Dad as kids – and it's a valuable lesson. I have known that lesson for so many years, but I sometimes need a reminder.

The experience of attending my 35th college reunion at Duke University had more impact than just a lesson about friends and family. More important to me, it was an honor to join over 100 of my fraternity brothers who had graduated between 1970 and 1979. I had not seen most of these men in 35 years.

I was a little surprised to learn the breadth of successes and failures in marriages, businesses, careers, and physical health. I think I expected that every one of these guys would be doing well and enjoying life, as I am, at least today. And many are. There are judges, lawyers, doctors, CEO's, and one guy who owns the best bar in Durham, NC! Some are in great shape, run every day, play golf, ride horses, hunt, fish, bicycle, whatever. Some are married for the first, second, third, or fourth (he married the same woman twice) time.

But many are not riding the crest of the wave of "success." Several have beaten cancer. Some are still fighting it. Some have broken marriages, bankrupted businesses, or both. But all are still trying, still competing in the game we call life. Somehow, we have all learned that there is nothing less important in life than the score at halftime. The first half is both passed and past. There is nothing that can be done to change it. What is important is focusing on what we will do differently in the second half – of our marriages, our careers, and our lives. There are no charmed lives. We all have our ups and downs, our successes and failures. When my Dad said "the sun don't shine on the same dog's ass forever," he was referring to both good times and bad. He wanted us to know that no matter how good we think we have it, it could very well change. And, no matter how bad we think things are today, with the willingness to work hard, a positive attitude, and persistence, things WILL change.

Tip: What, *specifically*, will you do differently today, tomorrow, next week, next month, and next year to make your life different? Change will come. What are you doing to prepare to persist?

Think in terms of the areas of your life that are most important to you. Reflect on your priorities and commit to changing something in your life to make it better.

Persistence

Start at the Top and Work Your Way Down –

I had the pleasure of working with Dad in the insurance business for 14 years. As was his way, he offered quiet support, preferring to stand on the sidelines and watch me. He was no different when I played high school football. During summer practices, I would look up and there would be Dad, standing on the retaining wall that skirted our practice field. He would watch for a while and then just disappear. I would look up and he was gone. I never knew when he was coming. I never knew how long he stayed. I sometimes didn't even know he'd been there.

He would come home that evening and we would all sit down to dinner. I learned very early on that Dad was not about to offer his thoughts about my performance or our team. He watched. He cared. He was there. It was the same way when I came to work in the insurance business after my six year stretch in the U. S. Air Force. Dad had little to offer in the way of advice. He was willing to answer any questions I might have, but for the most part he just watched, cared, and was there.

There were two things I heard him say more often than any other in those years. The first was "start at the top and work your way down." One of the most difficult things in sales of any kind is getting to the decision maker. In Dad's opinion, it made a lot more sense to spend your efforts developing relationships

Persistence

with the people in charge and letting them tell you who the decision maker was, especially if the top dog made the decisions.

It took some courage, or moxie as Dad would call it. It took some creative thinking to figure out how to get to that person. But in the long run, it was much more effective than being shut out by the receptionist. Dad's theory wasn't without flaws. I once sent a letter to, and then called on the CEO of a manufacturing firm in a neighboring town, only to find that she had died. Talking to her daughter who now ran the company was a bit awkward, but I did get to see her. She referred me to the family lawyer who was making business decisions on behalf of the family. He agreed to let me prepare a proposal and I eventually got the account. I started at the top and worked my way down.

The second thing that Dad said so many, many times was, "Pleasant Persistence!" I never heard him add anything to those two words. Just "Pleasant Persistence." Those two words were his words of encouragement. When I lost an account, or came in second on a proposal, Dad would give me that verbal pat on the back and remind me – "pleasant persistence."

My wife was shopping in the local grocery store, one of a medium sized chain in Indiana. She accidentally knocked a pop bottle off the shelf. It shattered on the terrazzo floor. A piece of glass ricocheted off the floor and cut her ankle, sending blood all over the aisle. The staff was efficient, caring, and helpful, applying a bandage and getting her to an emergency care center to get a couple of stitches. Within a day or two, we got a call from both the manager of the store and the insurance carrier making sure she was okay.

That's when I started asking questions. "Who is your insurance with?" "Who can I thank in your organization for such great care?" "Who is in charge of the insurance program for the chain?" Persistent question after persistent question eventually led me to the CEO of the grocery chain. After thanking him and complimenting his staff, I told him that I was in the insurance business too and that I really appreciated how well things had been handled. Then I asked if I could meet with him about submitting a proposal. He agreed to meet me, arranging to have his CFO join us. The next spring, I landed the biggest account I ever got. Dad was right. All it took was pleasant persistence.

Tip: When negotiating in business, and especially in sales, remember this acronym. Get the DIRTT!

D = Decision maker. Start at the top and work your way to the decision maker. Pleasant Persistence!

I = Information. Collect all the information you can possibly find. Pleasant Persistence!

R = Reason to work with you. Is there ANY reason not to work with you? Pleasant Persistence!

T = Time. Do you have enough time to do a professional job? Pleasant Persistence!

T = Trust. Have you established trust with your potential client? Pleasant Persistence!

Persistence

Chapter 6

SUCCESS

"The difference between successful people and those who are not, is NOT talent. It is the guts to move forward, to take intelligent risks, to try!" – James Bain

Success

Success and Happiness in Your Life –

There are no guarantees in life. We are all given a
native intelligence, some collection of talents, and,
hopefully, an environment that encourages our
development as human beings. It is what we do with
those building blocks that determines our success
and happiness in our lives.

Please understand that for many, the concepts of
success and happiness are not necessarily connected.
Many of us struggle for some definition of success,
even achieving it, all at the expense of being truly
happy. I believe you can have both. My Dad did, and
thanks to him and several other great teachers along
the way, so do I. It has not been easy, but it has
boiled down over the years to a pretty simple
formula.

First, ask yourself, why are you doing what you do?
Other than a paycheck, what is the reason you get up
or go to work each day? If you don't have a quick
answer to that question, you need to focus on your
Purpose. My guess is that, when you figure out who,
other than you, you are doing it for, you will have
found your Purpose. Look for opportunities to serve
others. Keep in mind that most of what gets done in
this world of any real consequence is done by average
people. Set your goals and be patient. Success will
always come to those who know what it looks like
and are willing to wait for it.

Second, make certain that you have invested the time, energy, and talent in preparing for the opportunities that come along. There are many people out there who seem to think that the successful and happy people among us got lucky. That's crap! They were prepared for the opportunities and took advantage of them as they came along. For every "lucky" heir out there, there are countless people who have come into money and squandered it. For every "lucky" professional athlete or entertainer out there, there are countless wanna be's who were not adequately prepared when their chance appeared. For every doctor, lawyer, butcher, baker or candlestick maker, there are countless numbers who have tried and failed, simply because they didn't prepare and have the willingness to do what it takes to get there.

Be Prepared. Learn something new every day. Read everything you can get your hands on. Learn to make adjustments on the fly. And listen – you might just learn something.

Third, make certain that you surround yourself with good People. Understand that good people may or not be in your family. You will need support and guidance from people who have a strong value system and who will be loyal to you. And you will need to be loyal to them. Recognize that people are different. That's a good thing. Believe in yourself and they will believe in you.

Success

Fourth, figure out what your Priorities are. Start with establishing your core values – those things you stand for and those things you will not stand for. Whether they make your core value list or not, consider the importance of respect for others, passion for what you do, and pride in your work as important values.

Fifth, be Persistent. Feeling sorry for yourself is a waste of time. No one else will, why should you? We all make mistakes. Get over them and move on. It's part of being human. Keep trying. It is after all the only alternative to giving up and that, simply, is not an option.

There you have them – the five P's. Purpose, Preparation, People, Priorities, and Persistence. It's just a model, but it has worked for me and so many of my clients – and it can work for you. It is your roadmap to success and happiness. Safe travels.

About the Author

Jim is a professional speaker, published author, and successful business consultant. A former principal in several different businesses, he has delivered presentations and been a featured speaker for the Associated General Contractors of America, the Mechanical Contractors Association, the National Electrical Contractors Association, the Construction Financial Management Association, and many other national organizations.

He is the Founder and President of the Falcon Performance Institute, a consulting and corporate training firm. Jim has a degree in Economics from Duke University and an MBA from the University of Puget Sound. Jim has been published across the continent in magazines such as *Tech Journal South*, *Practicing CPA*, *Looking Fit*, *Selling Power*, *Latin Biz*, *Business First*, and *Franchise Canada*.

Visit Jim's web-site at www.jimbainspeaks.com.